Simple Machines
Everywhere

Simple Machines in Your Home

Gillian Gosman

PowerKiDS press.

New York

For Roger and George

Published in 2015 by The Rosen Publishing Group, Inc.
29 East 21st Street, New York, NY 10010

First Edition

Book Design: Joe Carney
Photo Research: Katie Stryker

Photo Credits: Cover FreeBirdPhotos/Shutterstock.com; p. 4 V. J. Matthew/Shutterstock.com; p. 5 Darren Baker/Shutterstock.com; p. 6 Brian McEntire/iStock/Thinkstock; p. 7 Dorling Kindersley/Getty Images; p. 8 Rob Cruse/E+/Getty Images; p. 9 vinicef/iStock/Thinkstock; p. 10 Spike Mafford/Photodisc/Thinkstock; p. 11 Dirk Ott/Shutterstock.com; p. 12 Jupiter Images/Photos.com/Thinkstock; p. 13 Edsel Querini/iStock/Thinkstock; p. 14 Jupiterimages/Photolibrary/Getty Images; p. 15 photocritical/iStock/Thinkstock; p. 16 Miguel Lamiel/iStock/Thinkstock; p. 17 Rolf Sjogren/The Image Bank/Getty Images; p. 18 Medioimages/Photodisc/Thinkstock; p. 19 Amy Walters/Shutterstock.com; p. 20 Tetra Images/Getty Images; p. 21 ratmaner/iStock/Thinkstock; p. 22 monkeybusinessimages/iStock/Thinkstock.

Library of Congress Cataloging-in-Publication Data

Gosman, Gillian, author.
 Simple machines in your home / by Gillian Gosman. — First edition.
     pages cm. — (Simple machines everywhere)
 Includes index.
 ISBN 978-1-4777-6869-3 (library binding) — ISBN 978-1-4777-6870-9 (pbk.) — ISBN 978-1-4777-6644-6 (6-pack)
 1. Simple machines—Juvenile literature. 2. Machinery—Juvenile literature. 3. Dwellings—Juvenile literature. I. Title.
 TJ147.G687 2015
 621.8—dc23

2014001268

Manufactured in the United States of America

CPSIA Compliance Information: Batch #WS14PK5: For Further Information contact Rosen Publishing, New York, New York at 1-800-237-9932

Contents

What Are Simple Machines?

Your home is a place for sleeping, eating, and playing. It is also a place for doing work, though. You do work from the moment you turn the knob on your bedroom door in the morning until the moment you wash your toothpaste down the drain at night.

Homes are filled with simple machines. You can probably find a simple machine in every room of your home!

Kitchens are particularly full of simple machines. Many of the tools and gadgets kept in kitchens are simple machines. There are levers, inclined planes, and much more.

You do a lot of this work with the help of simple machines. Simple machines are tools that help us do work by multiplying or redirecting the amount of **effort** we apply to a job. There are six different simple machines. You will find many examples of each in your home.

Plane and Simple

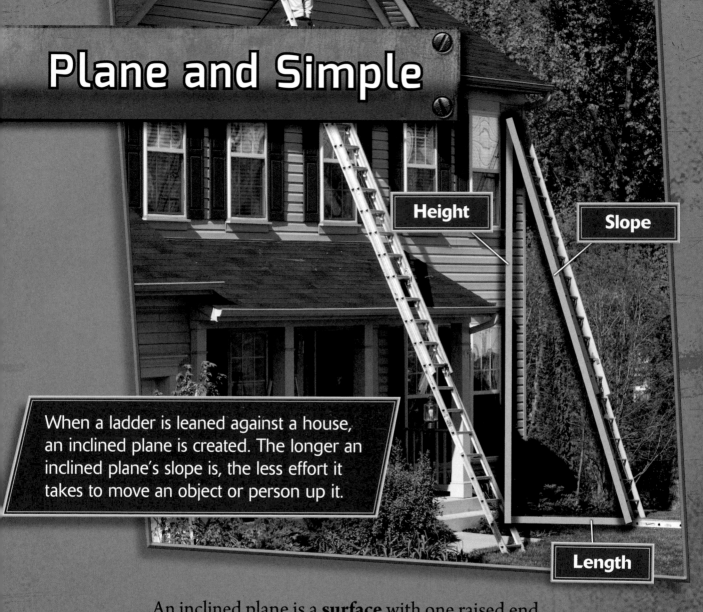

Height

Slope

Length

When a ladder is leaned against a house, an inclined plane is created. The longer an inclined plane's slope is, the less effort it takes to move an object or person up it.

An inclined plane is a **surface** with one raised end. We move objects from one end to the other end. Moving an object along the **slope** of the surface requires less effort, or **force**, than lifting or lowering the object.

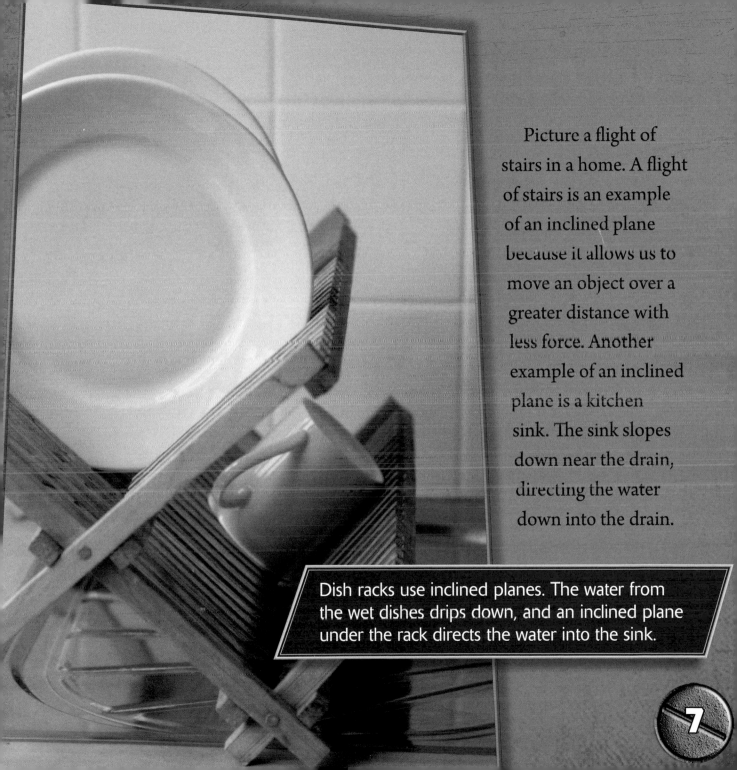

Picture a flight of stairs in a home. A flight of stairs is an example of an inclined plane because it allows us to move an object over a greater distance with less force. Another example of an inclined plane is a kitchen sink. The sink slopes down near the drain, directing the water down into the drain.

Dish racks use inclined planes. The water from the wet dishes drips down, and an inclined plane under the rack directs the water into the sink.

The Wedge Works

The narrower a wedge is the easier it is to push it between or into things.

A wedge is a tool with one **narrow** edge. The narrow edge is inserted into an object. The effort we put into driving the wedge into the object is multiplied and redirected sideways. A wedge can be used to cut an object or to hold itself in place.

A knife is an example of a wedge. Knives have sharp, narrow edges that cut through food or other materials around the house. A doorstop is another household wedge. The narrow edge is put under a door, holding the doorstop in place between the door and the floor.

A knife's narrow, sharp blade makes it easy to slice an onion. When you apply downward effort to the knife, it pushes pieces of the onion apart.

Effort

Such a Screw!

Thread

The thread around the base of a lightbulb screws it in and connects it to electricity, making the bulb light up.

A screw is a thin rod, or bar. A ridge runs around the length of the rod. This ridge is called the thread. One example is a wood screw, which is used to hold things in place. We apply force to the flat end of a wood screw, often with a screwdriver. The thread multiplies our effort. When the screw is in place, the thread serves as a wedge, holding the screw in place.

The threaded base of a lightbulb is another household screw. We apply twisting force to the glass bulb, and the threaded base follows the matching thread on the lamp's **socket**.

There are many items in a home that are held together by screws. Look closely at the furniture in your home, and you may be able to spot the screws.

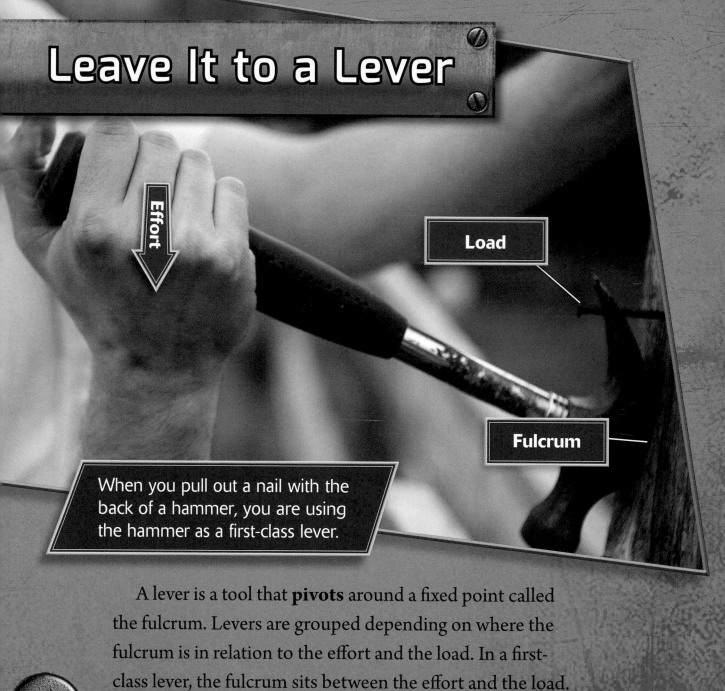

Leave It to a Lever

Effort

Load

Fulcrum

When you pull out a nail with the back of a hammer, you are using the hammer as a first-class lever.

A lever is a tool that **pivots** around a fixed point called the fulcrum. Levers are grouped depending on where the fulcrum is in relation to the effort and the load. In a first-class lever, the fulcrum sits between the effort and the load.

12

A hammer used to pull a nail up and out of a wall is a first-class lever. The nail is the load, and the fulcrum is the head of the hammer where it rests against the wall. The effort is applied by pulling downward on the hammer's handle.

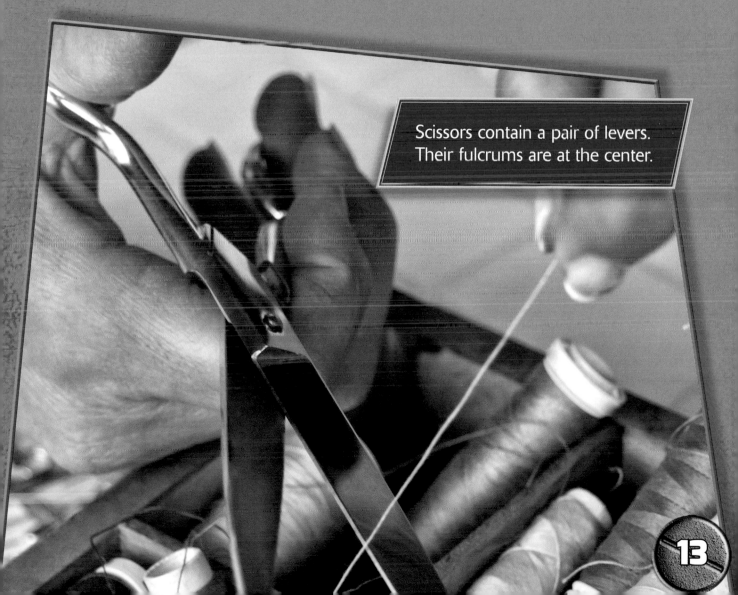

Scissors contain a pair of levers. Their fulcrums are at the center.

More Lever to Love

Fulcrum

Effort

Load

Brooms are third-class levers. The fulcrum is at one end, and the load is at the other. The effort is applied in the middle.

In a second-class lever, the fulcrum is at one end. The effort is applied upward at the other end. The load rests in the middle. A nutcracker is a second-class lever you might find in your home.

In a third-class lever, the fulcrum and the load sit at opposite ends of the lever. The effort is applied in the middle. A broom is a third-class lever. The load is the sweeping end, and the fulcrum is at the other end, which pivots in the upper hand. Effort is applied in the middle, where the broom handle is held by the lower hand.

Tongs are used for serving salads and picking up other foods. Can you tell what kind of lever they are?

Pulleys, Please!

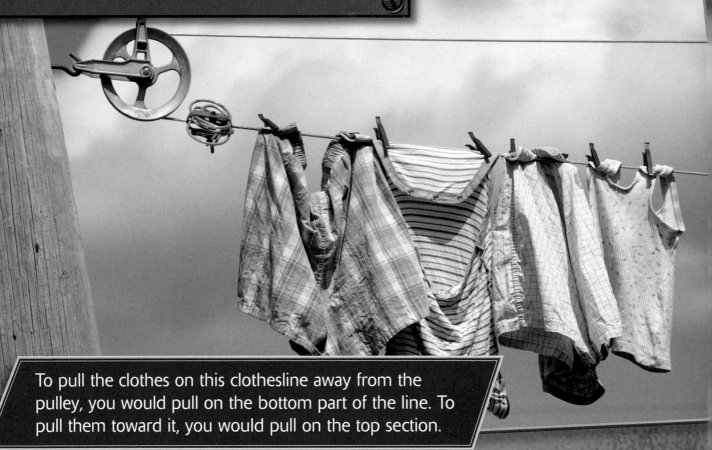

To pull the clothes on this clothesline away from the pulley, you would pull on the bottom part of the line. To pull them toward it, you would pull on the top section.

A pulley is a wheel that **rotates** on a narrow rod. A rope, chain, or cable runs along the grooved edge of the wheel. One end of the rope, chain, or cable is attached to a load. We apply effort to the other end of the rope to move the load. A pulley can be **stationary** or moving, and it can be used alone or in a **series**.

The window blinds or shade in your bedroom are moved up or down with pulleys. A series of pulleys connects the lift cord to the blind slats or shade.

A very small pulley can be found at the top of window blinds. When you pull on the string to raise the blinds, you are using a pulley.

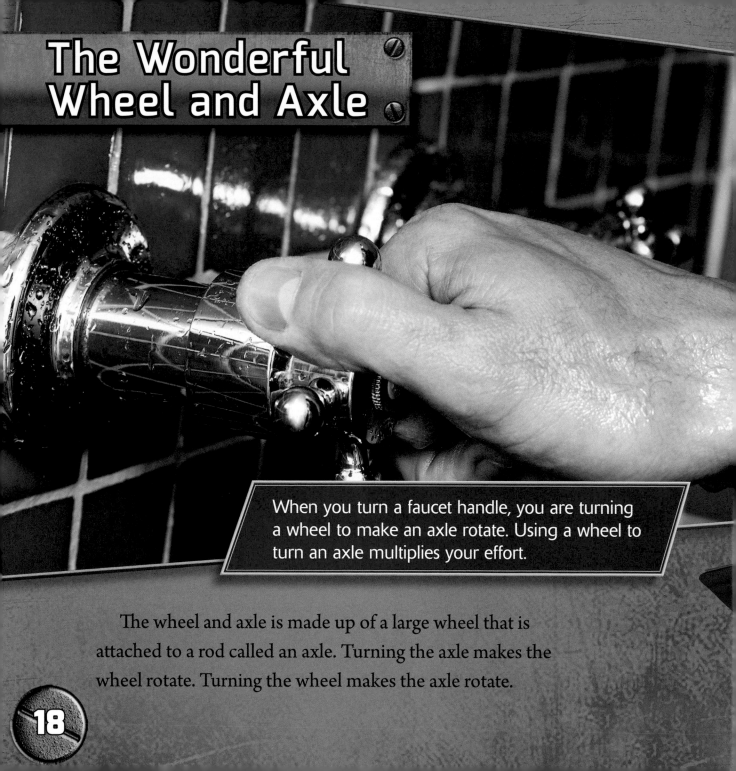

The Wonderful Wheel and Axle

When you turn a faucet handle, you are turning a wheel to make an axle rotate. Using a wheel to turn an axle multiplies your effort.

The wheel and axle is made up of a large wheel that is attached to a rod called an axle. Turning the axle makes the wheel rotate. Turning the wheel makes the axle rotate.

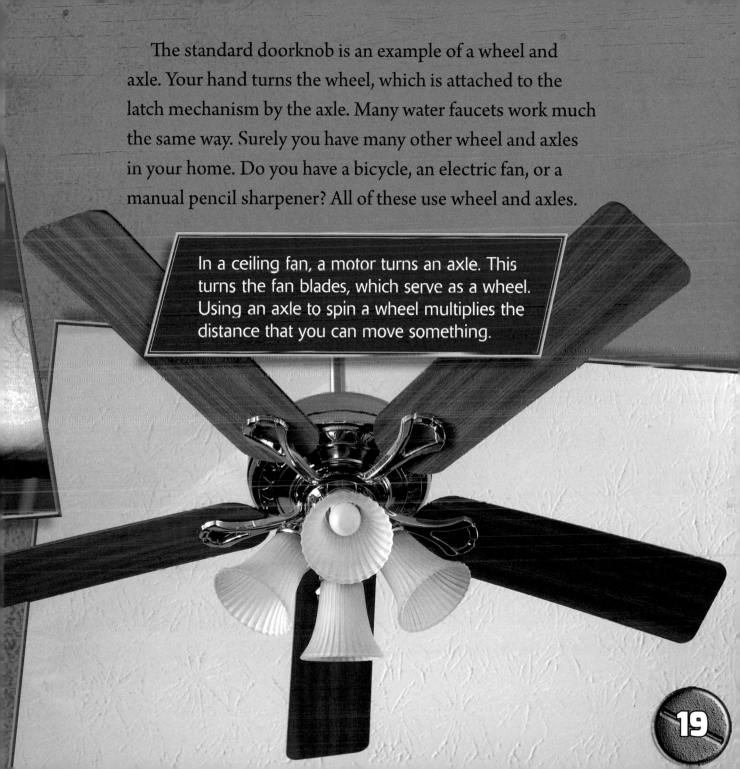

The standard doorknob is an example of a wheel and axle. Your hand turns the wheel, which is attached to the latch mechanism by the axle. Many water faucets work much the same way. Surely you have many other wheel and axles in your home. Do you have a bicycle, an electric fan, or a manual pencil sharpener? All of these use wheel and axles.

In a ceiling fan, a motor turns an axle. This turns the fan blades, which serve as a wheel. Using an axle to spin a wheel multiplies the distance that you can move something.

What Are Complex Machines?

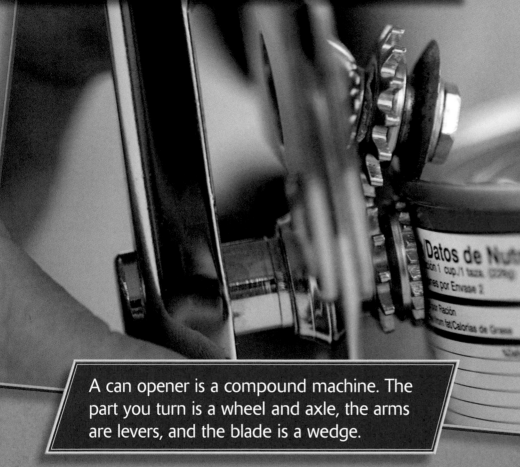

A can opener is a compound machine. The part you turn is a wheel and axle, the arms are levers, and the blade is a wedge.

Datos de Nutrición

When two or more simple machines are used together, the tool that results is called a compound or **complex** machine. Many common examples of simple machines in your home are, in fact, examples of complex machines.

Scissors are a common example of a first-class lever. The cutting blades also happen to be wedges, and the fulcrum is held together with a screw. The top arm of a stapler is a lever, while staples are wedges. Lawnmowers are compound machines, too. The cutting blades are wedges. On a push lawnmower, the handle works as a lever. On a riding lawnmower, the steering wheel is a wheel and axle.

A pizza cutter is a lever and a wedge. It is held together by a screw.

Helping at Home

Next time you are asked to lend a hand at home, remember the six simple machines that make household work just a little bit easier. After all, rolling the garbage can downhill to the curb, cutting coupons from the newspaper, and sweeping the floor all use simple machines.

Still struggling with a chore that seems too hard? Maybe you should invent the next great complex machine to tackle the job!

Simple machines help us cook, clean, and garden. What is your favorite household task?

Glossary

complex (kom-PLEKS) Made up of many connected parts.

effort (EH-fert) The amount of force applied to an object.

force (FORS) The power or strength of something.

narrow (NER-oh) Not very wide.

pivots (PIH-vuts) Turns on a fixed point.

rotates (ROH-tayts) Moves in a circle.

series (SEER-eez) Similar things that come one after another.

slope (SLOHP) A hill.

socket (SO-ket) The opening into which something fits.

stationary (STAY-shuh-ner-ee) In a fixed place.

surface (SER-fes) The outside of anything.

Index

D
doorstop, 9
drain, 4, 7

E
edge(s), 8–9, 16
effort, 5–6, 8, 11–16
end(s), 6, 11, 14–16
example(s), 5, 7, 9,
    11, 19, 20–21

F
food, 9
force, 6–7, 11

J
job, 5, 22

K
knife, 9
knob, 4

M
materials, 9

O
object(s),
    6–8

S
series, 16–17
sink, 7
slope, 6
socket, 11
stairs, 7
surface, 6

T
tool(s), 5, 8, 20

W
wheel, 16, 18–19, 21
work, 4–5, 22

Websites

Due to the changing nature of Internet links, PowerKids Press has developed an online list of websites related to the subject of this book. This site is updated regularly. Please use this link to access the list:

www.powerkidslinks.com/sme/home/